ISLAND

Wight to Kent.
Have a good
day
That complete collection
of SxL's is waiting
for you.

BY THE SAME AUTHOR

Householder
After The Deafening

ISLAND TO ISLAND

Gerard Woodward

Chatto & Windus
LONDON

Published by Chatto & Windus 1999

2 4 6 8 10 9 7 5 3 1

First published in Great Britain in 1999 by
Chatto & Windus
Random House, 20 Vauxhall Bridge Road,
London SW1V 2SA

Random House Australia (Pty) Limited
20 Alfred Street, Milsons Point, Sydney,
New South Wales 2061, Australia

Random House New Zealand Limited
18 Poland Road, Glenfield
Auckland 10, New Zealand

Random House South Africa (Pty) Limited
Endulini, 5A Jubilee Road, Parktown 2193, South Africa

Random House UK Limited Reg. No. 954009

A CIP catalogue record for this book
is available from the British Library

ISBN 0 7011 6869 2

Papers used by Random House UK Limited are natural,
recylable products made from wood grown in sustainable forests.
The manufacturing processes conform to the environmental
regulations of the country of origin.

Typeset by Deltatype Ltd, Birkenhead, Merseyside
Printed and bound in Great Britain by
Creative Print and Design, Ebbw Vale

For Suzanne and Corin

Acknowledgements

Grateful acknowledgements are made to the following publications where some of these poems have already appeared: *Ambit, Anthropology Today, The Observer, Stand, The Times Literary Supplement, Thumbscrew.*

'How to Trap a Giraffe' owes much to Alfred Gell's essay 'Vogel's Net' which appeared in *Journal of Material Culture, Vol. 1, No. 1.*

'The Swimming Match' is drawn from a similar contest in *Beowulf.*

The author also wishes to thank the Arts Council for the Writers' Bursary that it awarded to him.

Contents

MUSHROOMS OF THE SOUTHERN STATES

Suppose they'd always been there,
That this destructive mania
Had taken hold of Alabama
Like something in the water, the air.

Do they give a damn?
Apparent, like soft cromlechs
By Claes Oldenburg, or omelettes
From nature's own frying pan

And draped on trees, stairs,
These careless whispers of decay
Have penetrated Santa Fé
And built their plump acropolis.

It won't last. Mason–Dixon
Can survive these bloated husks
Of fly agaric as far as Texas
Each fall, until the next one.

ISLAND TO ISLAND

When Babelthuap was ants to its
Last square inch, we unhitched
The canoes we'd been carving
Since they first came and made for Ngulu,

The gods in our prow-boards and our hair,
And found girls costumed like men,
Hirsute with ants, so we rigged a sail
With their love and saw Sorol rise

Like the blunt skull of a terrapin.
There we found lawn-mowers but no grass,
The ants had finished every last blade.
A bathyscaphe bubbled up and two Russians

Mouthed smiling mirs through their round windows
As we paddled for Woleai, Faraulep
And Eauripik, realizing navigation was the art
Of avoidance, as it was the islands

That moved, not us. At Ifalik were bikinied
Mountaineers but no mountains
Save those built by the ants
Whose vice versa bodies peppered the beaches.

Beyond were bitty atolls, some entirely
The work of ants. We worried we'd
Take on their trivial concerns if we landed
But already talking was for us a kind of touching.

We saw the night drop star by star behind
Pigailoe, making us dizzy, and some of us
Strapped on paper wings and talked about
Founding a colony. Any infestation –

Of mice, of doubts, of spiders –
Will run a natural course. We were lucky
To have our islands, even when their geology
Pointed to pestilential origins

(Gaferut is a hornets' nest, Pulap not
Pumice but the guano of a billion
Pipistrelles). I developed
A native's love for these minor lands

And hope, as the last of Babelthuap's
Argonauts (my co-canoeists took flight,
Briefly, across the open sea), that I'll find
An island of solid sugar somewhere.

BEATRICE IN A BIVOUAC

Sugar-cube her some igloos,
Domed-ice mansions, and show,
Through sweet windows, views
Of uncomplicated snow.

Wig-wam her some willows,
Daub the wattle walls with shit,
Furnish her with skins and dead-leaf pillows
And nestle her there in rooms unlit.

Take sago palms and treacle canes
And lean them against a leaning cliff,
Start a fire of seaweed flames
And smoke her dinner in its drift.

Car-tow her in a caravan
Called Marauder, Viceroy, Jubilee,
Agrarian, Cygnet, Medallion
And leave her somewhere by the sea.

Huddle her in a sea-coast cave
On some ocean's southern shore,
Tell her quietly to be brave,
Part her shells and sweep her floor.

Show her to her shack, her shed,
Her den, her lair, roofed with earth
To house her when she's dead,
Then cover her with turf.

SUBURBAN GLASS

For example: conservatories.
In the alveolal cul-de-sacs,
Free from grass or anniversaries,
Of new housing estates, the backs
Of cornflake-orange starter homes tumesce
With glass – all-embracing windows,
Places where lives become less
Dark, and where geraniums grow.
Couples become biographies
As they plan their future flower-beds,
Waiting for their apples to be trees,
Turning yellow in their crystal sheds;
Marriages walled in by glassiness,
Set in ordinary palaces.

FURNISHINGS

He held the Chair of Falling Down,
Saying there is no life on the moon
But there is furniture . . .

He settled on a chaise-longue by Tycho Brahe,
He lolled on a settle in the Ocean of Storms,
He loafed on an ottoman by the Carpathians

Knowing how chairs were arguments
Against gravity, that finding the latent
Staircase in the cliff of oneself

Always means a moment of falling,
Of walking backwards, of finding
Gods in cushions, struts, upholstery . . .

So in the armchairs of the Lake of Dreams,
On the footstools of Copernicus, he sat
In the lap of the ghosts of astronauts,

Sharing a prie-dieu with the shadow of Pythagoras,
Little-finger-balancing chesterfields in Seething Bay
With the Earth overhead in its hammock of soot.

'This now is a place as well,' he said,
Arranging Hepplewhites for a parliament of dust,
'Where people end, furniture begins.'

A CHOCOLATE FIREGUARD

When he recovered he was full
Of tittle-tattle about the sun.
He'd been there, picnicking
In a shadowless landscape

With countless bleached
Divorcees furloughed from
Their lighthouses and bell
Foundries hypothesizing fish.

He was common knowledge
There in the manufactory
Of daylight and kindness
And promising personnel,

So when we found him
Gorging himself on iced
Water from the landing
Fridge we felt we understood,

Except that it wasn't a thirst
He was trying to satisfy,
But a memory, of blinding
Grass, surprisingly cool.

HOW TO TRAP A GIRAFFE

i.m. Alfred Gell

Oppose the empty time of waiting
Against a sudden catastrophe.
Egg the giraffe on
To complete a jigsaw
When he comes like someone
Certain he's not drunk
To the homely vicinities
Of the negative giraffe you've dug.

Convince the giraffe he's alone
By communicating a deadly absence.
Use the distance
Between him and his water.
Crazy-pave a lake
So that any descending
Head will be broken.

See the giraffe as uprights
In a world of horizontals.
Employ the poised violence
Of dappled javelins,
Broomsticks, ladders
And tent-poles,
Then pull away the rug.

Get the giraffe to be honest
About what he loves,
Then parody it.
A shower of nets.
A tree of arrows.

Imagine you are a giraffe
And send yourself postcards
Homesick for the veldt,
Filled with wish-you-were-heres.
End with the one about
The man who slipped
Into his bed
And never came out.

WOLF CHILD

Was it me you blamed
For your lupine manners,
Fierce at breakfast?
What brought you to our
Cottage? I thought you could be tamed.

Your brute tongue given the finesse
Of language. You would have been the last
Of your strange breed. I was a tower
Of strength at first, but waned
On touching your pelt's unusual fineness.

I put it down to a troubled past —
Wounded, limp, in the power
Of some running pack, your heart stained
By that tempting, glossy wilderness,
Life was something held in abeyance, a trust

Soon broken. Undreamt. Your paw
Scraped at the solid blocks of our books. I'd planned
An education for you, but those windless
Nights you howled at a bare bulb, or rushed
To the corner, gnawing at the floor,

Taught me you were more than could be tamed.
What was it brought you to our
Cottage, I thought, when, fierce at breakfast,
Putting aside any attempt at manners,
You told me it was me you blamed?

THE CATS IN THE CATENARY

Giovanni's skill is tail-
hanging the high
voltage cables
with a prehensile hold,
a gallows-swing, shock-proof,
O Gio takes, from the trains
passing under,
the thunder!

We are she-cats, he-cats, every-
cats, climbers of cedars,
eaters of fledgelings,
turned feral to breed
in these hanging gardens, the grey,
endless pergolas of the catenary,
better than trees
these gantries.

Locos whoosh. The pantograph
carries its bouquets of sparks
a hundred miles, our
uncles were chimpanzees,
we loris-grip the cables
upside-down, we've found our roots,
we purr and mew
at the two-two.

A commune. Cloud-cuckoos.
You'll see us slalom
through the latticed steel,
hiss electrically, spring
our claws at rolling-stock,
off-ground-touching. Think cats'-cradle,
scratching, spitting,
think knitting.

11

It's how we like to live,
in splendid insulation
in the horizontal rigging,
        we're Brunel's children,
Gresley's, Gio said so,
        we're danger overhead to the tok-tok
of a Bo-Bo
or a Co-Co.

These are testing times.
If you take the train
that plunders our attenuated
        country, watch for us –
on the slow camber of a bend
        we'll cluster on the wires like
monstrous crows,
        in rows.

We sense the least reverb.
We'll have you strung out,
we'll tightrope and tail-balance
        you out of your depth,
you'll walk a plank of air,
        fall to the clinker, the sleepers,
the rails.
We'll lash our tails.

AN ARABIAN DERBY

The air weighed tons.
The choked tannoys
Made it up as they went along.
Our boy, sesame-yellow, alone,

But burning to win.
The natural phenomenon
Of a date-palm oasis
Was the start and finish.

The course was dunes.
The race itself, just plumes
Of pink dust that, a week
Later, settled on Zamakh.

Part swans, part coconut shies,
The camels had the shambling poise
Of reservoirs of calm
Balanced on a frantic scrum.

We passed round aubergines and felafel
While taking in the awful
Truth about the course –
It wasn't ours, or was,

In a sense, everyone's.
The race's history had undone
Countless billions of grains
Of our land, the race remained,

But our land had changed,
The kicked-over ground, churned
Like bread, like rice,
We were the course, we were the race.

Hamum came home first,
His hair was pink and stiff.
Our boy, sesame-yellow, delighted,
Took his prize of tabbouleh, and ate it.

COW PATS

They mark the sites where grass
Withdrew and turned it on itself.

A kind of writing, like Verloc's
Boy outlining his life

With compasses, endlessly.
This must be Giotto's own dung.

Settlements of flies, peculiar
To cow pats, thrive, quora

Of ginger executives in committee,
Planning their pasts. Step

In one and you might fall
For ever, right down to the first

Blade that dared root.
And a season's grass rises

In lush domes where the cow pats were.
I think of the shabby crowds

Of grass queueing to leap
Through the black hoop of a cow.

The grass somersaulting.
The cows turning somersaults.

Our baby son somersaulting
In his own sienna manure,

Making dirt impossible.

ONION

O onion, in
Slicing you
I've the XXIIIrd

Olympiad. Track
And field. One
On one on

One. In
A persistent
Vegetative state

I've fried
Hoop-la
And won

An orrery.
Wheels
Within wheels,

O wheels O
Onion, who
Winds

Your clocks?
No one no
One.

CHEF

Is food an illusion?
I thought so once
When it was revealed

Our head chef
Was an ex-conjuror.
In his sanitized

Environs he stood
White as an Alp
When I saw him

From the tumult
Of a rolling boil
Lift a live chick.

What went on
In the dark theatres
Of his ovens was

The same secret
Process. 'It is a matter
Of faith that food

Tastes,' he said, sawing
In half a halibut
That later he made

One again in the milieu
Of a bouillabaisse.
'Chefs save us

From the agnostic's gruel,'
(Bringing butter to hazelnut,
Flames in the stalls applauded)

'The world,' he said, laughing,
'Beneath the sealing crust
A magma of steak and kidney.

Life begins with soup,
Like dinner. Boys
Of the world know it.'

I couldn't argue.
Our guests were disappointed
With his rabbit en croûte,

Searching for the meat
In a top hat
Of puff pastry,

But were delighted
By his speciality –
Dove pie.

After the first
Slice the doves
Kept coming.

THE TAXIS

I saw the taxis
Flowing like treacle
Through the Kentish Styx.

Their fares were people
Injured by minicabs –
Enfants mutilés, cripples,

The lame, the lost, the handicapped.
The taxis turned
In a blaze of hub-caps,

Flags, streamers, balloons,
Through the mysteries
Of orchards, the North Downs,

To the sea, the sea
And all its brittle edges.
The rides were free.

REVOLUTION OF THE VIADUCT

I've no bridge,
Just domed air, no bridge
From which to view the moonsets, worldsets.

(Paul lived
In the third alcove, lived
In a monumental mantelpiece

On a diet
Of sugar-loaves, a diet
Of ghostly sugar-loaves, he lived

On a bridge
That wasn't there, a bridge
Of air and air, in a big country.)

We've no bridge
On which to be anywhere, no bridge
To span a moraine, or flood

A defile with bricks,
No sky of arching bricks,
But doors, or doorways, or doorframes,

Sequential exits,
Entrances and exits,
We can't know which is which.

WRIST

Carefully adjusting your watch,
Instead you've freed that
Complimentary red balloon
You'd looped there on leaving
The eatery and which now
Dithers, a tiny pulse,
Above the town. And you
Are left to remember how
It was anchored to that
Universal joint whose arcs
And leverage now amaze you,
Your hand's own neck,
Scented isthmus, with its
Branching maze of blood
Where every turn is the right
One. And you recall,
Then dismiss that thought
You'd had of opening it,
Letting all those lanes
Merge into one awful junction.
It took on, briefly, the qualities
Of your entire body, dancing
In handcuffs, hooped
With your identity tag.
Better to bracelet it
With a bubble of helium,
Let your heart lift
With it. Your watch
Wasn't even there. Won't
Be now. But you'll look
For the time in your skin.

THE CAMOUFLEURS

I

Of course, you wouldn't
Know they were there.
You shook when you saw

The forest up and leave.
And then, in an empty room,
Realized it was crowded.

But think of the bombers.
At night they imagined
Our country was back

In the dark ages.

2

They were the true
War artists. A drape
Of scrim and the factory

Was pleasant summer days.
They smeared black
Over our bright faces

In the theatre of war.
And one did landscapes
In between battles,

In camouflage paints.
I said to him, surely
There was a city there,

A church at least.

RECENT HISTORY

Having filled the space
Between the event
And its recollection
With an album of feathers

Found in a birdless city,
Hadrian left Antioch
Trailing the exclamatory
Quills of magpies.

Architecture is politics
By other means,
He thought, and saw,
In the structure of feathers,

A possible future
For buildings – slim towers
With floors pinioned
On a single hollow stem

With syphon-powered
Paternosters. And further,
Feathers themselves as
The supreme building material –

Downy courts, pillowy piazzas,
Fluffy, snug palaces and theatres
Vapid, deep, cosy,
With walls full of give . . .

This in a man so concerned
With outlines. He defined
The empire with a fringe
Of limestone, ancestor

Of plumage. He saw it
As a massive wall of feathers,
Blown away on Pictish breezes,
Reappearing, much later, as history.

THIRST

What they didn't know
When they wrapped her,
Stalling each finger tip
With gold, each nipple,
Folding together a makeshift
Phallus just in case,
Giving her back her legs
In cedarwood, her feet
(Rushes woven with reed –
Ends arranged like toes)
Was that her empty
Yet meticulously complete
Body was only one
In a crowd of strangers –
The beetle *necrobia rutipes*
From a stray cup of water
That had found its way
To her lips.

MOUNTAINOUS

Even as boys we'd loved
The risky puppetry
Of mountaineering, being
Each other's hearty scaffolding,
Finger and toeing the overnamed
Fissures for our pointed trophies.

We'd learnt an alphabet together.
All As. All upper case. Our lives
Were at right angles to other children's,
So that when he slipped that one
And only time, thirty years later,
Letting out a cry that went
'Marthaaaaaagh', resounding about
The St Virtue Pass for a full minute,
Shove-halfpennying the eagles from their
Poised eyries, he said it was
His weakness for grand gestures
That led to his fall, my fondness
For understatement that broke it.

But why, on that zig-zag
In the granite we called
Totentanz, did I prize
Out his pitons with
The penknife we once shared?
And why did his saved life fall
So silently past me?

THE CONTESTANTS

The contestants faced
Each other. The first,
Pulling his lower lip up
Over his nose,
Posted himself
In the envelope of his person.

The second, not to be outdone,
Grinned, knowing that his ears
Were the recto and verso
Of the book of life.
He too could shut
Himself up in a pamphlet
Of his own skin.

In the way that embryos
Form through folding,
Like the making of beds,
Of beds within beds,
These senior citizens
Seemed to have found

A long-lost elasticity
To life, latching
On to the very origin
Of movement, of life
As motion, of faces
That meant anything.

After an hour of eyes
Staring from between
Ancient lips, or of
Tooth enamel gleaming
From the pink extravagance
Of an eye-socket,

The contest climaxed
When both widened
Their throats so far
Their very heads
Seemed to dangle
Over the warm abyss
Of their peculiar ambition.
And then it happened

As it had to, when
The westerlies shifted
And they crossed that line
Dividing face from fantasy,
Somehow they fell into themselves
And now inhabit a world
Of unstructured smiles
And meaningless frowns.

And I think of them
As two gardeners
In a garden of pink
Roses trying to get
The flowers back
Into the buds.
I thought of them
In the butcher's
When the butcher's
Gold wristwatch
Slipped and fell
Into a tray of hearts.
I think of them now.

PRECIOUS

When they fished you out of the green channel,
Gutting your luggage, excising that red
Number you'd cha-cha-cha'd in, I spun you
Off to twirl in a stark ballroom and passed,
All clean and innocent, through Hounslow.

Like the harlequin bringing up an illness
Of bunting, or the lady and the tramp
Kissing in the same length of pasta,
I remembered the look you gave me
As you downed those hot bundles, that later

Showed up like a white choo-choo stuck on a
Hairpin of peristalsis, a cortège
Of drowned sorrows — in all those greys
Of your anatomy, so legible.
I'd rumba'd with a collage of x-rays.

Why did we foxtrot so much that trip?
How far did we quick, slow, quick quick, slow?
Why did we samba and tango and conga
As if our lives held no tomorrows?
Our steps could have paced out a

Pilgrimage to a motionless shrine, I thought
At Acton Town, while you sat on Marat's
Lavatory, not recalling the jiving lurches
That had you falling through a gloomy shaft of me.
They'd lit you like a pumpkin with sterile torches.

Nothing shone back. I was at Leicester Square
When they undid your shit with shrink-wrapped hands,
And pigged out on tacos at Chi-Chi's.
Your razzamatazz of gems looked dull and suburban.
My tongue had turned blue as a chow-chow's.

IN THE MUSEUM OF PURE MATHEMATICS

It reminded me of the couple
Whose love-making involved
A thin plastic tube
Connecting their urethras

And the subsequent exchange
Of the contents of their bladders
For up to a dozen times,
That day we considered

Sex in the Science Museum,
Amongst five floors of inventions
But best against the glass
Case of Babbage's Difference

Engine. There was no difference
When they discharged that final
Liquid into a beaker of home-
Blown glass and savoured

The aroma of pi calculated
To the billionth place.
We would have got further
Had the attendant turned his back.

ON THE BATTERY FARM

You loved me here, once,
Among the sheds of the philoprogenetives.
Our brief marriage flared
Against the astrophysics of egg
After egg ad infinitum.

I remember the day you came –
Me on a roof twisting the louvres
Of a vent with a monkey wrench,
You with the grotesquerie
Of your rucksack packed with fir cones.
You'd strayed from your arboretum
Into my 'Avian Auschwitz'
I think you called it.

And I shinned down to give you
A guided tour, thinking you'd love it
Like I did. I showed you how silence
Has a soft hubbub at its heart,
How the unfertilized ova trickled
Down cushioned chutes to land
Plumb in the nooks of cartons
Recycled from cashed gyros. Our hatcheries

Had you clapping your hands,
But they were over your mouth,
Your ears, your eyes in our trim
Slaughterhouse with its humane
Spark. 'It's as though they've
Given up.' You never got over the shock.

And now I'm left to think about the things
I could have done to make you stay:
Entertained you with nights of risky
Juggling; the egg, glass, coin
And piece of string trick; the overnight
Miracles of whisks and omelettes
Tangential to each other.
I could have travelled with my eggs
To another dug-up Arcadia,
Chucked them at the hard hat

Of a contractor. But it was gallinaceous
Salvation you were after. The revamping
Of a lost generation. You would have
Stripped my agribusiness bare,
Given cruel half-flight to orange
Clouds of hens. 'Hatch! Hatch!'
You gnashed in your sleep.
Perhaps we should have had kids.

THE HANDSTAND SUMMER

We lived in a one-way street,
But that didn't stop the cars
Cheating on dark nights.
I blamed the girls

Who'd been practising
Handstands all summer,
Egging each other on
Until they could kick
Themselves into the upside
Down in one movement.

It became normal to see
Feet sway like ripened
Corn past our window
And hear the clatter
Of heels as uprightness
Regained itself.

By September there were
Formation cartwheels,
Synchronized handsprings,
And we got so used
To the summery arcs
Of young feet behind
Our television, so used
To inverted footprints up
Our flank wall
That going to sleep
I really felt I might
Wake on the lunar
Landscape of our ceiling,
And it took all my
Concentration to prevent

My tea swelling
To a brown uprising.
I considered painting
'This Way Up' across
The front of the house,
I considered posting
A wine glass
And an umbrella
At the gateposts
As reminders of the rampant.
But I wondered if even
I could get enough sense
Of the perpendicular when
I was besieged by girls
Taking the world
On their shoulders in their
Bluebottle ambitions.

What world did they
Have in mind
I wondered. I found
Myself being sweet
To them, thinking
Of a place where houses
Hung like the last leaves,
Where the ground was a deep
Lake in which we
Would never drown.

THE SWIMMING MATCH

You'll remember our swim —
Doing battle with the swarm
Of water, dressed in sure-sink
Armour, dressed like tanks,
Swords held in both hands,
Our crawl cut our earth-bonds.

A week we were on those straits.
How we longed for the feel of streets.
Our floating became a daily grind,
Our feet never touching the ground,
O for grass, trees, walls, a cliff,
Anything but that violent surf.

And you, rusted, kelp-strewn,
Collapsed on that other coast alone,
Boasted you'd outswum me,
That I'd failed in the spumy
Channel. You let them think
That somehow I'd sunk.

But I was moving in a bubble
Of my own steadfastness, able
To out-think seabed monsters.
While you were lying to ministers,
I was clearing lanes for shipping,
Cleaving Leviathan, outstripping

The kraken. My sea-strength was greater.
The real battle you'd only passed over.

DARK BATH

Stepping into the bath
'I've abandoned ship,' you laughed,

So when the lights
Fused that night, the ship

Became all too real;
Splish, splash, house,

Ocean, ship. I shouldn't
Have laughed but fished

The lukewarm seas
For your body, sent

A midget-sub of soap
To find the worst

When all seemed lost,
Or hoped a fleet

Trawling the limits
Of its field might

Drag you in with the cod.
But I knew you were

Still there. You shouldn't
Have laughed as my ship

Went down, nor held
The sponge aloft

Like that, getting
Blood out of a stone.

THE MADNESS OF HERACLES

I

Yawning she was merely mouth,
A plush tongue fenced in
By snowy weaponry like the lounge
Of someone important, so that
To sleep there meant
To sleep soundly. At the back
Beneath lierne vaulting
A tunnel issued lengths
Of breath and the voices
Of the still-living people
Of Nemea who moaned like food
Won't. Closing her mouth,
Eyes lazily closed as well,
She sat. Twelve hands
To the shoulder, a mane shaggy
Like the glamorous collar
Of a woman from Hollywood.
Fur so thick swords and arrows
Were pins. A hide the colour of
Strong tea, a tail like an individual
Python with a ball of fur
At its tip from which one blow
Would negate all golfers instantly.
He had his work cut out (he
Loved his work). His knife
Bent like airline cutlery,
His club was tooth-picks after
One blow to that magnificent head.
Man to man, face to face,
A thing so tough
Only its own teeth and claws
Could pierce it, like the genius
Whose only possible downfall
Is her genius. Wrestling
Was the only option.
They waltzed for a moment

Like Androclese until
Their dance took to the throat
And the lion was strangled.

At first he boasted
In the pubs of the Peloponnese
Demonstrating his massive
Grip on the willing barmaid,
Opening packets of crisps
In the manner of prizing jaws
Apart. He ransacked the salt
And vinegar and swilled
His lager like the blood
He'd drunk. But now he wears
Her pelt and sits like a
Huge tom and finds he has
Become cat-like, restless
On the back streets. Kids
Call to him 'here kitty kitty,'
Prowling queens
On the backyard walls
Or under parked cars,
Drop their scent and he sniffs.

II

Face to face to face. The first,
Something she left on the pillow,
A depression where she'd slept
Face down, that deep concavity
Was her nose, this the soft bowl
Of where she was with even a trace
Of foundation, of lipstick where
Those lips kissed nothing all night.
Later I found the place she made
Up, a desk at which to write
The colours of life and see them
In three mirrors, and the apparatus,
Oily pencils, powder puffs, little
Chimney-sweeps' brushes for re-
Sooting the lashes. She had
The works, was an artist
Of some sort. A former lover
Had done her bust, the bastard.
She has it in the garden
Mounted on a plinth
And made to look old with sour
Milk. It was her thirty years
Ago. But no colour, of course,
Apart from the colour of stone.
A bird uses it regularly as a site
Of ritual defecation. Bless it.
A robin, I think. Leafing
Through a book on a villa
That somehow survived I saw
Her face again, this time
Constructed of a thousand
Tiny chips of stone, a masterpiece
Really, shining after a thousand
Years in deep dirt, but she
Was some deity that once
Belonged to the river Darenth

And had fresh water loaded
In her breasts that spilt
To be the river. Face
To face to face. The nearby
North Downs I decided one
Morning were her brow, that
Former buttress of an arch
That once had Kent propped high
On the ex-seabed. I thought
Of bone, and when the orchards
Ripened I saw her face again.
The cherry tree grew frighteningly
Tall, like cherry trees shouldn't,
Their fruit lethal if it fell
On you. But they were her lips,
I knew, and the leaves as well,
Her face was made of the orchard.
This was the fifth face. Our window
Cleaner came later, noisily
Happy he wiped our glazing
And it streamed. She came in crying
Like an echo of the house, like the house
Had managed to invigorate a piece
Of itself. What about her ears,
I wondered, was this something,
A door into darkness, that I
Could explore. Then I
Saw her face in a fold of folded
Curtain, and wondered if I had
Seen something new for the first
Time, or if it was like firelight,
The face you couldn't help seeing.
I saw her face covered in face pack,
Given a skin-tight mask.
I wasn't expecting it, that face,
Those ovals around her eyes, two slices
Of cucumber giving her a green glare.

I kissed it and woke up with mud
On my lips. That was it.
Face to face to face.

III

Some of us run for a living,
She, for instance, who darted
Like something in shoes
Designed by the farriers
Of Oenia, so swift she
Could catch herself at the tape,
A hind of such beauty,
Four legs better than two,
Standing out from a beautiful
Breed. She let grow from her temples
Two crescents as if a honey
Moon had pierced her head
To leave a tip each side.
Her flanks were like light
Through beech trees with
Even moss hinting at a mature
Decay on her splendid legs.
And when she moved, beginning
With a leap that was like
Waking, or a sector
Of trees had decided to live
Like us, I followed, and she
Ran for her life – it was
Her living – swerving, hop-skip-and-
Jumping, doubling back, short-circuiting
The whole of Arcadia in the orbit
Of a gnat a million times
Its size, right up to Istria
A year later when, both of us
Panting like failed commuters,
I found her beneath a wild
Apple tree, her legs giving in
At last and the flies gathering
About her flickering ears.
I shot her through once
Without wounding her, piercing

The gate of bone and tendon,
Carried her back like a Spanish
Lover, to Mycenae. How did I manage
To out-run my love, to be marathon
Gold medallist a thousand times
Over? It was the retreating
Face that got me, the look
Over the shoulder, the come-on
That made me want to know her
Better. I won Mastermind
Over and over, and every
Game show going, became
Professor of everything,
Finished crosswords just by
Thinking, not writing, could recite
Books I'd written without writing.
It can get you like that. The hardest
Questions had the simplest answers.
How do we know our mothers?
How does gold get into the ground?
I'll tell you.

IV

He thinks of him every
Morning between shaving
And leaving. The fireworks
In the frying pan, the salt
Residue like undigested
Milk curdling with the fat,
The rind, the tough edge
Of life with painters'
Bristles still there, here
And there, on end as if
In shock. A memory stronger
Than buildings, grass will be
Where the snout now troughs
Through filth. And the children
Making pyramids of children,
Where the apex never is
Because kids aren't bricks
But fall like all of China
Jumping off a chair.

She was a deity to whom
A shower of gold
Was small change, something
Filched from the money-
Box. That time she lifted
Her apron up to the waterfall
And became pregnant with river.
It set him off on long
Weekends in Arcadia hunting
With the lads for stags
And boars. 'Don't come to me
When you feel the pennies
Pinch,' she said as he left
In a vessel to bob upon
The briny, the undefeated
Sea, to him a thousand

Prisons built of salt,
Jostling. They'd dissolved
In the rain and pickled
Fish now leapt the brooks
Of fresh water. He remembers
An English river and its nymph,
Twin rills babbling
From her breasts. She
Made him feel so thirsty.

V

Noisy. Those lesser redpolls
Raise havoc in the catkins
And have ruined the farm.
The farmer can't sleep,
His wife milk or the kids
Hike through their favourite mud
In case the lesser redpolls snow
Their poison excrement and
Freeze them sadly in the middle
Of play. A single flock
Might take a day to pass,
Be visible from space. And noisy.
Deafening. It is a song they
Keep up only on the wing,
Their dipping flight, underwriting
The air like finches will, statements
Made and emphasized.
The river bank's Piccadilly
Circus now or a trench
On the front line. Even the rooks
Have given up hope – I saw
Their bleak procession
Heading east yesterday.
Give me a pine forest
Of conifers unlimited,
Give me the gloom of spruce
And larch where no
Birds sing, not these
Fruitful thickets. But it is
South and deciduous
And home to an old
Cacophony, a din,
A ding-dong, ding-a-ling,
What a racket!

But it wasn't them. Instead this man
Shaking his rattle worse
Than a baby and the air
Was instantly thick
With finches' wings,
A flutter of eyelids, awake,
They took to the sky
In clouds like Leicester Square,
Dirigibles of birds passing
In and out of each other,
Dividing, merging, shapes
That made us think of songs.
They gave a naked tree
Pink foliage suddenly.
He chased and raised
His superior din and the tree,
Our favourite old ash,
Shattered, as if a dog
Had shaken off its water.
They thickened the copse
By living there for a minute
But he chased again
And so it went, this
Endless removal, abridged
Migration, from tree
To tree, one forest after
Another until he was at
The beach and made
Dry land intolerable.
They had no choice
But seaward and so
Flew their twittering, dipping
Flight above the crests,
Became a hazard
To channel navigation
For a few days, a treat
For the few birdwatchers
Left in our world.

I couldn't accept it
Entirely, as if a piece
Of our country had disengaged
Itself, as if a hazy
Laputa had levitated,
As if an offshore rig had
Longed for a berth
In a sheltered cove.
He kept his rowdy vigil
Up and down the south
Coast until with aching
Wings the lesser redpolls
All at once perched
For ever on a wave's bubbling
Summit. A day later
The tide left them deep
On the beach, knee-deep,
And heavy, you wouldn't believe,
As if the ocean couldn't handle them.

VI

Up to our knees. The world itself
Given a muddy face. The stratum
Of filth became strata
And built a motionless
Machine that no one knew
How to work. Except
The bluebottles who saw
It's possibilities. Risky insects,
They gambled on the chance
Of civilizations built on dung
In which they could have government.
They met at the gorgeous
Nostrils of cows
Who'd never known illness
And dreamed long dreams
Of their black, teaming cities.

Men tried to find a use as well –
One saw designs for artificial
Foods, another thought,
Condensed, it could
Be bricks, or honed further
Into special jewellery. And,
Of course, another saw gold.
It was a waste of time
And time itself came
In reeking drops and slowed
Down till it seemed the day
Had lost its insistence,
Had become one with yesterday,
The weeks and years were all
A semi-solid heap of the vile.
We could smell the humus
As we sat in our useless
Villages, clouds
Of dirty cumulus forming.

The real clouds gave up.
One just hung for days
Over the clock, refusing
To rain.

So he delved
And cut into the river,
Rode it, as it were, harnessed
The flow with reign
And bit and led
His liquid nag forth from
Its ancient bed. The crowds
Of bulls that chaperoned
The messy cows fled
The one pouring hoof
After another. Trod. Gods
Wept. A thousand new
Waterfalls were born
That day, and I loved
Being soaked for the first
Time. For the first time
A good day was a bad one.

VII

In my distant memory, a woman,
A son that might have been,
A charming hybrid chewing
The cud with intelligence,
Fashioning things out of the earth.
Her bed was the softest
Ground I'd trod in a lifetime
On my feet, like grass
That's outgrown lawnhood.
It was as if my wife
Was down to her bones, the elegant
Skeleton, but soft, and I didn't
Know if we should mount
Like I was used to, or if
I should graze her, because
There was something of grass
About her as well, a triangle
Of black turf, but we hardly
Fitted. I stood and wore
Her for a moment on my
Cock, like some tribal
Chief whose gourd is a measure
Of his power. I was doubled,
I admit, just for a moment,
And she shook like a local
Earthquake beneath me, a small
Disaster as I sneezed into her.
That is all in the past. A distant
Memory. My son as well,
The human piece of him
A hideous deformity. Never
Mind. I headed north and found
New pastures, sent shepherds
Scattering, or were they
Bishops? (Later I kept
Having this dream about

A golden shepherd all
Jewel–laden and richly
Encrusted who seemed
Willing to forgive whatever
I did, so I toasted him
With my voice and ate
Him. Very tasty.) Orchards underfoot,
Vineyards went. Only the farmers
Touched the tips of my horns
For good luck. I let them. Well,
What else could I do? Later
I was captured much to my
Dismay by a man half my
Size, chained and
Conveyed across the seas
To Argos (not the catalogue store)
To find that I was a gift
All wrapped in prettily
Decorated paper. It was dark
In there but she broke open
The gift wrapping to reveal
All, me, in other words. I promised.
I offered her new children,
A family. 'Bullocks,' she said, 'I'll
Not have my household overrun
By steaming little cows and bulls.'
What prejudice in one so
Beautiful. But she didn't
Want me anyway. I was set
Free and roamed south through
My lovely Arcadia again,
There to cut the lonely
Blades and garnish with my breath
The sweet herbs and hills
Before yet another hero
Came. It was in Marathon
Not long after, another

Big timer, big shot,
Who fancied his chances,
He got me by the horns,
Rode me like a bicycle
To Athens. I won't tell you
About what happened next,
Or what's going to happen.
I could make them kings.
Take my crown, I told
Them. Why won't they?

VIII

Cannibal mares. They bellowed
In their dreary manger.
I smeared the sleepy grooms
With blood and they dozed
Heavy on their charges' sides.
It wasn't quite the Derby. I
Harnessed four and rode them
As one, until I was set
Upon by others wanting
Their horses back. Podargus,
Lampon, Xanthus, Deinus.
Later they ate their masters
While the flesh still lived,
And not for the first time
I found myself an itinerant
Zoo-keeper, animal handler.
It was their ferocious appetites
Their masters satisfied
And they became docile
After that and turned
To grass, a new delicacy
Underfoot. They let one blade
Thrive into a tree and then
Lived in its shade. Not for
The first time. Nor the last.
I listened at the door
Of every stable I found, their
House, the horse looking out
Like a dreamy proprietor.
But there was always
A storm in the offing,
Threatening weather,
Mysterious meteorological
Phenomena, warm days
Never ceasing, clammy
Cells packed with golden,

Glittering honey, as if their
Larder promised food for ever.
I came back to the start,
Sculpted a horse in stone
And then three more, fitted
Them together to make
A quartet of horses
Playing at oneness, rearing,
Bucking, despising reigns, bits,
Harnesses or girdles, they cavorted,
Galloped, trotted and pranced
Like dressage, like very small
Horses, like ornaments rather
Than horses, like jewellery based
On the horse, like flies
Rather than horses (a train
Of them steered themselves
Between my breakfast
Plate and my breakfast
Cup) like the word 'horse'
Signifying something unequine,
Like dust rather than horses.
When the bonfire had finished
The specks of horses came
Floating down slowly for days,
Dirtying the washing. And so
In this world horses became
A logical impossibility.
Nights she clutched the lush
Floral extravaganza of her
Eiderdown, wondering at that
Receding sound in the lane,
That valedictory clip-clop.

IX

If clothes were all we wore.
But it is much more than that.
I came up with a bra
Based on the principles
Of the cantilever bridge.
Undressing was really
A means of getting back
To the beginning. It was her
Origins and I was her archaeologist.
I cut into a squared-off part
Of her and found the entrance
To the tomb of a big man,
A hero from a long-forgotten
Civilization. We opened
This together, drew everything
We saw, recorded and analysed
It. I didn't realize, having
Not reached very far, how
A person is layered: skin, fat,
Muscle, organs, bone, like
The strata of our world.
We considered the weather,
And the origins of weather,
How the atmosphere is layered,
A sequence of gasses with the thin
Membrane of ozone like
The skin of air. Satellites
Passed in and out of our
Thoughts. The moon passed
Into eclipse and then
Out again, and we considered
Space and the origins
Of planets, and how our
Solar system is layered.
The sun a sort of bright
Stone at the centre of

A huge, black fruit,
Its frozen rind only
A remote idea. And I
Considered how this poem
Is layered, each line
Uncovering the next
As though it was undressing
Itself and the last line
Would have verse in all
It's nudity. And that
Was when I came across
The statue. In the centre
Of her body there was
An art treasure, a figurine
Of great antiquity that
Still needs to be documented.
It meant I had to go naked
Through the streets.
I ransacked the washing lines
And whirligigs for lingerie. I
Waited patiently by the portholes
Of washer-driers in the coin-op.
A moment's indecision and the door
Opened on a tide of silk underwear
Flowing over me. Afterwards
They looked like the Alps
Dissected, a geologists's
Exploded view of mountains
To show their history. Those
Matterhorns. That Mont Blanc.

X

Animal husbandry. I'd had
Enough of it, even as I crossed
The world to the west to
See where the sun sank
And the inconceivable ocean
Beyond. But enough of all that.
The sun was unkind to me,
I developed a heat rash
And tried to kill it,
Make it set for ever,
And as an apology it leant
Me something from its
Dining table, a golden
Cup. I was chastised
And sailed the choppy
Straits like a true salt,
A navigator. I was wester
Than ever. And laughingly
I killed the Jack Russell,
The Royal Jack Russell
That came yapping
Across the pastures.
And then the herdsman came
Tending his red flock.
He went the same way.
I felt a little sorry for him
But when I saw his charge,
That blood-red herd, the crimson cows,
Bulls and heifers lowing
And chewing, I prized them
Above everything, and their
Owner, a man of impossible
Anatomy — three heads,
Three bodies, joined at the waist,
More hands than a dealer
At the casino. It took

Just one arrow to pierce
Every part of him, so long as I
Got the angle right, but I'm good
At that sort of thing.
It's my living, after all.
And so the journey back.
A difficult one by any
Standards, with all
The pestering by milkmaids,
The constant search for grass,
For new pastures. We nibbled
A swathe across Europe,
All through, until
The dairies were gone,
Daisy, Christabel, Annie.
In one place I eliminated
All cicadas, stopped them
From singing right away,
They don't sing there any more,
They don't sing. I was left
The sole dairymaid, I had
To milk them myself, that
Was the problem –
I'm not much of a hand
When it comes to the delicate
Work like that. I found
It quite a chore.
But I'm not complaining.
There were other things
I had to do, like tether
My ropes up to the bleeding
Cows themselves. Very hard
To loose them in green fields,
They were visible for miles
And they terrified the villagers
Who thought them some
Sort of demon fresh

From Hades. But they
Were gentle beasts,
Only interested in grass,
Really only interested
In what was right under
Their noses.

XI

No cake, not even a horseshoe
Of coloured paper, but a pip
Spat out from a magnificent apple
Was the only gift at their wedding.
The pip regained the tree
It fell from and resumed
The apples, the sole bower
In that lovely garden west
Of here, in the Atlas Mountains.
I found my way there
By picking a God out of his
Current and shaking him dry.
He sprayed river everywhere
Like a dog before directing me
And then I found that unusual
Garden, Eden's prototype,
With a serpent coiled round
The trunk of its only tree,
Guarding the fruit thereof.
I asked Atlas to get the apples
For me, but he said he was scared
Of this dragon, so I shot it
With an arrow over the garden
Wall and then took the vault
From Atlas and carried it myself.
The whole weight of the heavens.
I was surprised how light
It was actually, stars are not
That heavy after all. But that
Was the hardest bit. I didn't
Want to carry them for long.
I remember apple scrumping
In the vicar's garden before
The war. It was like that,
Come to think of it, creeping
Into someone else's garden

In the dark, plucking three apples
One by one. He came back
And tried to get out
Of taking the world back,
So relieved was he that he
Wanted a little longer
Without his burden. I thought
That if I agreed that would be
The last I saw of him. I'm not
Averse to a bit of hard work,
I can muck in with the rest
Of them, and if it comes
To that I can have the whole
World in my hands, you and me
Brother, for as long
As it takes, for ever if need
Be, but anyway, fair's fair,
So a bit of an argument ensued,
And Atlas, the pest, ran off,
And I couldn't chase him,
Bent double as I was under
The constellations, or I would
Have dropped the whole firmament
And Orion would have come
Toppling down on us, ready
To cause untold commotion. So
I reasoned with him, proposed
A fair exchange of apples
For stars. A fair day's
Work for a fair day's pay.
He thought about it, considered it
For a while, and then resumed
The journey, passing back
Over the generations
For hundreds of years
Until we decided we
Were different people and had

In us the possibility
Of whole races, gave birth
To China, Egypt and islands
As yet unconquered somewhere
In the South Pacific. I saw
An old man in young man's
Clothes, a cow lowing by the sea,
A lizard in agony on the hot
Cement, half an owl, just
The top half, as if it had
Been sliced in two, and unusual
Weather all round.

XII

Mad dogs. Dangerous dogs. They have
No place amongst us. Even if it
Was proved that a good dog can
Do no wrong and that its
Habit of killing is the result
Of selective breeding, I would
Still say that it can only be
For the good of the community
That all dangerous dogs are
Rounded up and banished
To a lonely island. The Isle
Of Dogs. And so I crossed
The dark river, frightening
The ferryman just by looking
At him. I didn't need
To go so far but on the left bank
I met so many known strangers,
So many faces familiar from
History that I felt that
Somehow I'd come home, was
Back at the very beginning,
The start of it all, and that
I was moreover glad to be
Back. It didn't last.
The entente cordiale was broken
By the first spear thrown
Of the afternoon. It passed
Painlessly right through me
Leaving not a mark, though my heart
Did register something as the harmless
Spike pierced it. A ghost
Spear, spear of mist, cloudy
Weapon thrown by someone cloudy
As well. I greeted them all
Like abandoned cousins before I came
To my senses and found

That I wasn't where I thought
I was. Later on that same day
I descended, steps leading down
Deeper into the world itself,
Corridors unlit, vestibules
And cloakrooms haunted by hissing
Overcoats, and at the door
To the loo I saw him, on guard,
A crazy dog with three heads
Issuing a dog noise in triplicate,
Then he bit me in triplicate,
And went off on his cacophony
Of victory, singing like Peter
Pears. We danced a dangerous
Dance for a moment and then
I hugged him like a lover
Until his breath was all but gone. I felt
Like a new man, lugged him up
To the surface and questioned
My ability to train even the
Tamest of dogs, let alone this brute.
But he succumbed, was soon rolling
Over for Bonio, shaking hands
Embarrassedly, fetching sticks
Like a real retriever, even
Balancing on his hind legs
And staggering for the benefit
Of assembled people. But he'll
Be up to his old tricks
Soon enough, I fear. He has
Me round his little finger,
Knows exactly when I'll be home,
When I go to work, when
The dustmen come.
He knows his place now,
And I know mine, it's
The same — everywhere.

And I love my dog.
Workmen drop their hammers
When we pass by. The streets
Are empty for us,
And the parks. The triple
Echo of his voice has Gods
Shaking. They shout,
'Dangerous dogs! Dangerous
Dogs!' And he, 'Woof, woof,
Woof woof. Woof woof.'